When Parents Split Up...

HOW TO KEEP YOURSELF TOGETHER

By Alys Swan-Jackson

**With material from
Lynn Rosenfield, L.C.S.W. and
Joan Shapiro, Ph.D**

Illustrated by Andy Cooke

PSS!
PRICE STERN SLOAN

For my mother

Acknowledgements

Thanks to Hampstead School, East Chester High School,
The Bronx High School of Science, Parliament Hill School,
and the individuals who kindly completed the questionnaire,
and to the following individuals and organizations
which supplied reference material and advice:
The Brook Advisory Centre, The Philippa Fawcett Library,
Simone E Katzenberg (Solomon, Taylor, & Shaw, Solicitors),
Relate and The Trust for the Study of Adolescence

Text copyright © 1997 by Alys Swan-Jackson. First published as *Caught in the Middle* by Piccadilly Press Limited. *Help : A Special Section* copyright © 1998 by Lynn Rosenfield, L.C.S.W. and Joan Shapiro, Ph.D. Illustrations copyright © 1998 by Andy Cooke. All rights reserved. Published by Price Stern Sloan, Inc., a member of Penguin Putnam Books for Young Readers, New York. Printed in the United States of America. Published simultaneously in Canada. No part of this publication may be reproduced, stored in any retrieval system, or transmitted, in any form or by any means, electronic, mechanical, photocopying, recording, or otherwise, without the prior written permission of the publisher.

Cataloging-in-Publication data is available.

ISBN 0-8431-7451-X (pb) A B C D E F G H I J
ISBN 0-8431-7461-7 (GB) A B C D E F G H I J

Plugged in ™ is a trademark of Price Stern Sloan, Inc.
PSS! is a registered trademark of Price Stern Sloan, Inc.

CONTENTS

INTRODUCTION

More than seven million American kids and teenagers have divorced parents. That's a huge number. But when it happens to your family, you can feel very alone.

In this book, you'll hear from lots of teenagers whose parents have gone through a divorce. They talk honestly about the feelings they had during this difficult time. They tell exactly how they coped and what they did to help themselves.

In some families, the separations were friendly and carefully planned. In others, there was anger and violence. But no matter how "good" or "bad" the divorce, all these teenagers had a time of feeling deeply unhappy.

Dealing with a breakup is never easy. You have to remember that it's not just a single event but an ongoing process of readjustment. But, like everyone who contributed to this book, you can do more than just survive. You can come out feeling good about yourself and your future.

ONE

BREAKING UP
IS HARD TO DO

Finding Out

Did you have any idea your parents were splitting up? Even if you suspected, finding out for sure can really hurt. How did they break the news?

I asked

"I heard my mom tell my dad she was taking the dining room table with her. That was weird. I asked what was going on, and that's when they told me. I remember saying to myself over and over, 'Everything will be okay.'"

April (13)

They told me

"I wasn't surprised they split, because they'd been arguing a lot and not really speaking to each other. After they told me, the tension at home got worse, because my dad didn't want to move out and my mom was really unhappy because she wanted him to go, and they were arguing about that, too. It was like a war zone."

Peter (13)

3

"I was going to a movie with my friend Jane, when Dad said he had something to tell me. He said he was going to move out. He and Mom thought it would be better if they lived apart."

Louise (16)

Mom just left home
"I'll always remember the day Mom left. Dad took me and my brother to the park, and when we got back there was a note on the kitchen table from Mom saying she had left home."

Ann (17)

I overheard a conversation
"When I went to bed, I could hear my mom and dad talking. I heard my name a lot, and I knew I shouldn't have, but I listened outside the door and I realized they were talking about divorce. Soon after, my mom told me she and Dad were splitting up. I didn't let on I knew anything, but it really hit me then that Dad was going and might not come back."

Miriam (17)

"I wasn't that surprised, because I'd heard them talk about separating before, but I was surprised because they hadn't been arguing that much recently. My dad told me that he was looking at an apartment to live in. They had intended for my mom to tell me, but it hadn't worked out. I felt really upset and shocked."

Louise (16)

Although it seemed to Louise like the end of the world, it wasn't. The same will be true for you. No matter how bad you feel, it will get better.

For most parents, their kids will be almost the first consideration when they discuss splitting up. They will do the best they can for you. Divorce is tough on everyone, but you can come out of it stronger and smarter than you were before. As you read this book, you'll hear from other teens and just how they got through it.

First Reactions

"They were always arguing, so I was relieved, really. At first I felt sad that they couldn't be together, but I thought that from now on things can only get better. At least they won't be at each other's throats all the time."

Louise (16)

"I was furious. I thought, this isn't supposed to happen. I screamed at them, 'I hate you, why are you doing this to me?'"

Paula (15)

"I was stunned. I woke up one morning and Mom had packed up and left. Dad only told me when I asked where she was."

Nina (14)

As you can see from these teenagers, initial reactions to the news can be very different. No matter how much you expected a split, it's always upsetting when you're actually told. Most people take their parents' being together for granted, and something you've always taken for granted has come to an end.

Were You Kept in the Dark?

"It was obvious that something serious was happening. Things had begun to go rapidly downhill between my parents. However, nobody told us. We felt like we didn't exist."

Olivia (15)

Naturally, you want to be told what's going on right at the beginning, and to find out what's going to happen to you. However, lots of parents find it hard to explain to their children why they are splitting up, and may not talk about how the split will affect you. Why? There can be many reasons.

- They might feel they are protecting you by not discussing the breakup. Parents often don't realize that teenagers have a lot more understanding than they're given credit for, and are mature enough to make their own judgments.

- They may not be aware how much you need to know what's going on.

- They are probably having such a hard time themselves that they haven't stopped to think about how you feel. It could be that your parents are under so much stress that they can't focus on you.

- Some parents feel guilty because they think they've let you down.

- There might be so much hostility that they can't even talk to each other to discuss what's going to happen.

Getting Answers

The best thing you can do to get as much information as possible is to ask your parents what is going to happen. Make sure you pick a convenient time—not, for example, when your mom or dad has come home exhausted from a hard day at work. If you don't know how to begin, say something like "Mom (Dad)—there are a few things that have been bothering me. Can we talk?" Explain that even if they can't tell you immediately, they need to keep you informed so that you will feel less confused and afraid. If talking to them is difficult, try writing them a note explaining how you feel and what you need to know. Try to include some loving words in it—they probably need as much reassurance as you do at this time. And don't be afraid to tell them what you want.

"It took a while for me to understand that Mom and Dad were so upset about the split themselves that they forgot that we were hurting, too, and needed their support."

Carla (14)

Talk to Me: Questions Teens Ask Parents

♦ Why are you splitting up?

♦ Will your separation be temporary, or permanent?

♦ Are you going to get divorced?

♦ Is either of you going to marry someone else?

♦ Where am I going to live?

♦ Which one of you will I be living with?

♦ Will I still be able to see the rest of the family—grandparents, uncles, aunts, etc.?

♦ Will I have to change schools?

♦ What will I tell people who ask what's going on?

You can write your questions down so that you are prepared and don't forget anything. Writing is also a good way to let your feelings out and to help you decide what you need.

Talking and listening are the keys to communication, but neither is easy to do when everyone seems to be on opposite sides or on the offensive. Don't give up. Asking questions helps you deal with your feelings of fear and uncertainty. These feelings aren't going to disappear unless they are faced head-on. Not only will you feel better, but your parents (and other people) can help you more if they know how you feel; the average person isn't a mind reader. By listening, you can see your parents' problems from their perspective, which will help you to understand everything. Try to keep a calm head and an open mind.

Remember that your parents might not answer all your questions right away. Be patient—in time you'll find out what you need to know.

"At first I felt as if I'd never be normal and happy again. But I was wrong!"

Emily (14)

TWO

BEFORE THE SPLIT

"I think the worst thing was how much they hated each other and how mean they were to each other all the time. They were always arguing and carrying on, big fights that would end with one of them storming out, banging the door behind them. I really hated it, and I couldn't do anything about it."

Michael (18)

Conflict between parents is very hard for teenagers to deal with. It is the most upsetting part of life before, after, and during a divorce or separation. Even so, lots of kids wish their parents would just stay together.

"I kept thinking, if only we could go back to the way it used to be . . . I forgot the bad stuff."

Jenny (16)

Was Life Before the Split Really So Great?

It's easy to blame everything on your parents' splitting up and to think that if they hadn't separated, you'd be happy.

Be honest. Do you remember life before the split as totally great? The chances are it wasn't. Everyone has to face family problems of one sort or another. Since your parents were unhappy, life before the split was probably tough. Unhappy parents may do all these things:

- ◆ Fight
- ◆ Leave the room
- ◆ Refuse to speak to each other
- ◆ Always give in to the other's demands in order to keep the peace
- ◆ Scream and cry
- ◆ Get depressed
- ◆ Drink, take drugs, or overeat
- ◆ Try to blame the problem on the other parent
- ◆ Get involved with someone else
- ◆ Resort to physical violence

Here's what some teenagers remember.

They were always arguing

"My parents were always arguing. Mom yelled at Dad; Dad went out, slamming the door. It seemed sort of normal. Then one day Mom and Dad sat us down and asked us how we'd feel if they split up. I was amazed."

James (15)

"My mom and dad were always fighting. It was a real shock

when they decided to divorce, but it was a relief, too."

Jane (15)

If your parents always had fights, then you might not have realized that anything more serious than usual was going on.

Fights can occur in all kinds of families; in fact, some families seem to thrive on them. Fights help clear the air. They can be the first step to problem solving.

However, if the fights are very frequent or very unpleasant, they are a sign that something is wrong. Sometimes parents can be getting along so badly that they use any excuse for an argument.

"My parents always argued some, but then they started going over the top. They were really getting on each other's nerves. I think it was when they had a massive fight about Mom leaving some potato peelings in the sink that I realized there wasn't much hope for their marriage!"

Jade (18)

My dad used to beat up Mom

Physical abuse is very serious and very scary.

"My dad used to beat Mom up when he was drunk. I didn't know what to do. I wanted to help her, but I just buried my head under my pillow and pretended nothing was happening."

Donna (14)

Jane's parents' relationship had been teetering on the edge for the last year. Both of them were holding down high-pressure, high-power jobs. They barely had time for each other. They didn't talk for days on end, and when they did, it ended up as a shouting match, with each one hurling abuse at the other. Eventually, things came to a head.

"Mom discovered Dad was having an affair. She overheard him talking on the phone to his girlfriend, and that was it, really. They had a big fight, really physical. Mom beat Dad up pretty badly. She kept hitting him with a wine bottle. I couldn't bear it. I wanted them to stop, but I didn't know how to stop them. That fight was the first time the subject of divorce came up.

"Mom and Dad could see I was upset. They said that whatever happened, they'd see I was okay and that they would go and see a counselor person, who would help them decide what to do."

Jane (15)

Lots of kids feel, like Donna and Jane, that they should have been able to stop the violence. They need to understand there's nothing they could have done.

They hardly talked to each other

In many ways, the worst kind of "not getting along" is when parents just don't communicate with each other at all. They avoid each other's company and don't speak to each other. Sometimes one of them always goes along with what the other one wants, just for the sake of avoiding any confrontation. Silent parents can mean there's an unbearably tense atmosphere at home.

"I couldn't stand it. Dinner time was the worst. My mom had this frozen smile and was very polite. Dad only talked to me or my sister. I'd eat as fast as I could so I could get away from them."

Julie (14)

I thought they got along really well

Usually, if you think back to how your parents were getting along before the split, you'll remember telltale signs that things weren't good, even if you didn't notice them at the time.

But maybe family life felt really normal and your parents seemed to be getting along fine. If so, the split may be particularly difficult for you.

"My parents are splitting up. It's a real shock. I thought they got along really well. They never had fights. Mom always did what Dad wanted. I don't understand why they're splitting up."

Chris (15)

Sometimes parents seem fine in public, even if they're obviously not getting along so well at home.

"I'd lie in bed listening to them shouting, but I didn't think it

was that bad. They never argued in front of me or Grandma or anyone. They acted like normal, although it was obvious it was kind of a strain. It never occurred to me they'd break up."

Paula (15)

Trying to Save a Relationship

Is it possible that your parents could still stay together?

Usually the answer is no, though you may feel that if your parents approached the problem in the right way, a split could be prevented.

There are ways of dealing with marital problems, if the couple fail to resolve them by themselves. It can be valuable for them to seek the assistance of a third party. This person could be a family member, or a mutual friend, or a marriage counselor.

If your parents have just split up and they haven't sought the help of a counselor before, it might be worth suggesting it to them.

A counselor got them talking

Problems never get resolved unless they are forced out into the open. The only option is to talk about them, no matter how unpleasant and depressing they might be. It's often helpful to talk to someone who's completely objective, and here is where a counselor comes in.

The counselor won't necessarily help your parents stay together. If it's clear that there's no way of saving the relationship, or if either of your parents is absolutely set on separation, then the counselor will assist them in making the split as easy as possible.

"My parents went to see a marriage counselor, who got them talking to each other again. It didn't stop the divorce going

ahead, but at least it was less nasty than it might have been."
John (16)

Trial separations

Separation and divorce are different. If your parents separate, they will usually live apart, although they might, generally for financial reasons, continue living in the same house.

Some separations are temporary. They give a couple a chance to think things over and decide what they want to do. It is a good time for them to go to a counselor or group counseling. If they decide to get back together, the absent parent can simply return. Separation is difficult for kids because they feel that their parents are neither married nor divorced, and they can't be certain what is going to happen next.

If your parents do have a trial separation, you should realize that they're unlikely to get back together. Because you (and any brothers and sisters you might have) are involved, most parents will have tried everything first and decided to separate only as a last resort.

Once your parents have thought it through, they will reach a decision. If they decide to divorce, then you have to accept that there's nothing you can do to bring them together again. Instead, try to concentrate on yourself and your feelings.

THREE

IF ONLY I'D . . .

Even though, deep down, you probably know you're not responsible for your parents' splitting up, it's really common for teenagers to feel that, somehow, they might have contributed to the breakup.

"The worst thing was the hate between them. They really hated each other. All they'd do was put each other down to me all the time. I hated being caught in the middle of it. I couldn't stop them. I tried to tell myself it's not my fault, but I couldn't."

Rachel (16)

Why Teenagers Feel Responsible

Life is very complicated when your parents are breaking up. On the one hand, you are probably feeling relieved that a long period of fights and tension is over, but on the other hand, you're hoping that your parents will work it out and get back together. Even if they were fighting, at least they both were still around. Then you have to face up to the fact that the separation or divorce is going to go ahead.

Why has this happened? Was it my fault? Was it something I did? are typical reactions.

If only I'd done what they wanted

"My first thought was, this is all my fault. I remembered all the times I'd argued with Mom and Dad and carried on if I didn't get my own way. If only I'd done what they wanted, this would never have happened."

Darren (16)

"My parents separated when I was sixteen. It seems ridiculous now, but when Mom left, my first thought was that I should have done better in my school. She was really upset when I got bad grades, and I said to myself, if I'd worked a little bit harder, done a little bit better, she'd never have got upset and left us like she did."

Michael (18)

Mom blamed me

Sometimes, in an angry moment, one of your parents might have said something like, "No wonder Dad didn't want to hang around when you're so moody all the time,"or whatever. At this emotional time, it's, sadly, not surprising when parents (or anyone else involved) say the first thing that comes into their heads and which they don't mean.

They argued about me

"I was quite a rebel, and my parents were always arguing about how to deal with me. When they told me they were getting a divorce, I just knew it was because of me, and I felt terrible. Then I talked to Grandma, and she told me that they'd just have found something else to argue about if I hadn't been there."

Jade (18)

I kept asking for things

"I felt really guilty. I knew they were having money problems.

I thought, it's all my fault because I keep asking them for new stuff."

Peter (13)

As a teenager you're more likely to feel responsible than if you're younger. For one thing, teenagers often have emotional relationships with their parents. Teenagers also make more demands: You want to go out with your friends, you want to buy clothes, you want to stay out later. But however much you have infuriated your parents recently, you certainly aren't to blame for the failure of their relationship.

Why It's Not Your Fault

The only people who are responsible for the split are your parents.

Your parents are adults, and their relationship is separate from yours, so no matter how difficult you might have been, you couldn't have caused the break. Remember that the split is between your parents, not you and your parents. Your parents' love for you is unconditional; their love for each other is not. Unfortunately, many parents will be so stressed out that they may not show that they love you. Try hard, if you can, to let them know that you love them.

Getting Guilt-free: Strategies to Help

◆ Write down the reasons you think your parents are splitting up.

◆ Pick out all the things you think you did to cause the split. Write them down, too.

◆ Look at your lists. Think of what you might have done differently. Would that have helped?

◆ Ask yourself honestly if you are involved. When

you think about it, you should realize that nothing you did could have affected your parents' relationship. Would you really have had that much influence over your parents? It's more likely you share Donna's experience.

"My parents never let me do what I wanted, so I gave them a bad time. My friend, though, she was good as gold. It didn't do either of us any good. She never got her way either. And both our parents ended up divorced."

Donna (14)

If you still believe you're responsible, you should talk to someone who can give you an objective opinion. They may help you see that it's not your fault.

FOUR

WHY RELATIONSHIPS FAIL

"Mom told me she never expected to get divorced—but she stopped being happy with Dad."

Jean (14)

When they first get married, a couple usually has the best of intentions. Very few people make commitments without truly believing and wanting them to last forever.

Even Your Parents Were Young and in Love Once

There are lots of reasons why couples decide to get married in the first place. Usually it's because they feel they are in love. They get along very well and enjoy being together. They are attracted to each other. They have similar ideas about life and what they want from it.

You can probably think of loads of other reasons, but as you can see, none of them is necessarily permanent—couples can fall out of love; sexual attraction can fade; goals can change; once they really get to know each other, they can discover they are actually very different people . . . .

It's worth taking a closer look at some of the reasons couples split up.

They drifted apart

"My mom and dad both worked really hard and they both liked doing different things when they had any free time. They told me they'd just drifted apart without really realizing it and

didn't have much in common anymore."

Sarah (16)

When relationships do break down, the people involved often don't realize anything is seriously wrong until it's too late. Maybe they've refused to acknowledge the problems.

They've started to lead separate lives, and one day one or both of them just decides they shouldn't be together anymore.

They couldn't handle Dad's being out of work

"My dad lost his job a year ago. He hasn't found another job and he just hangs around the house all day, watching TV. My mom hates it. She's always after him and complaining about how we can't have things because there isn't any money."

Warren (15)

Parents have to have a strong relationship in order to cope with difficult times—like money shortages or a severe illness. In such situations, marriages often either collapse or get stronger. And if a couple is already having problems, pressures of any kind can be the last straw.

Mom and Dad never saw each other

Many couples find themselves working long hours in order to afford a good standard of living, often at the expense of their families. Karen's father had a job that meant a lot of traveling. He was hardly ever at home. Karen's mother went along with this arrangement, but kept hoping that her husband would work in a less demanding field. One day Karen's dad told the family that he had taken a job in another city and that they all had to move. That was too much for Karen's mom, who decided she wanted to separate.

Mom met someone else

Sometimes a parent may have had an affair or have met someone else. That doesn't necessarily mean she or he wants to break up. However, the other parent might feel very betrayed and want the marriage to end. On the other hand, your mom or dad might think he or she can lead a happier life with the new person.

"Mom told Dad she was having an affair, and then he moved out. He hates her now."

Kim (14)

"Dad took us out to dinner and said he was sorry, but he felt he had to leave. He was in love with someone else and couldn't live without her."

John (16)

Dad's an alcoholic

Alcohol or drugs can lead to all sort of problems, including violence.

"My dad's an alcoholic. Mom put up with his drinking for years. Then one night he got so drunk he nearly killed her, and she threw him out."

Stephen (16)

Although it may seem obvious to the outside world that the best thing is to get out of an abusive relationship, the people involved often find that difficult and frightening to do. Sometimes the abused parent thinks that he or she can help the partner change. It can take a long time for a parent to accept defeat.

"Dad always liked a drink, but then he started drinking really heavily. He'd get drunk and pass out somewhere, and me and my mom would have to get him and bring him home. I think that's the reason my parents split up."

Tina (15)

Adults—Tina's dad, for example—may use alcohol, drugs, or food to help them cope with stress. If you see that your parents are hooked, you will have to accept that there is nothing you can do to make them kick the habit. No amount of begging, crying, or protesting is going to work. However, don't ignore it. Never cover up for them or make excuses for their behavior. Deal with your own feelings instead. If you are feeling angry or ashamed, you can seek the help and advice of organizations such as Alateen, which was begun specifically to support the children of problem drinkers. You can find a list of some of them at the end of the book.

They each gave me a different reason

"What really upset me is that both my parents gave me totally different reasons for the divorce. I was very confused. I thought, 'which one of them is lying?' If my parents could have given me good reasons why, instead of just blaming each other, I would have felt far less hurt."

Donna (14)

Perhaps there really are a lot of different reasons why your parents are splitting up. It might be difficult for both of them to put a finger on one specific problem. But if you are unhappy about anything you've been told, asking one or both your parents is the best thing to do.

They won't give me a reason

"I wondered why my parents were breaking up. They just said, 'You wouldn't understand.'"

Julie (14)

If your parents either refuse to talk to you or don't give you an explanation that satisfies you, you can talk to someone who might be able to help—a grandparent or a family friend, for instance. Remember, though, that your parents are entitled to privacy, just as you are. Also, it may not be totally clear even to your parents what went wrong.

Don't Take Sides

It's easy to take sides when your parents split up; it's extremely easy if you're closer to one parent than the other. Of course, that means you might get a very one-sided view of the split.

If one of your parents has met someone else, is an alcoholic, or has an extremely difficult personality, for instance, you're likely to blame that parent for the split. But remember that only your parents know what really went on in their marriage. There may be a lot of problems that you know nothing about. What is important for you to understand is that your parents still love you, even if they are no longer in love with each other. You don't owe one parent more loyalty than the other. Try to concentrate on *your* relationship with each parent. That's what is important.

Most couples who split up finally separate for good a year or two later. By then they are quite sure they will never get back together again. If they believe that the end of the partnership is for the best, you have, whatever your feelings, to accept it.

FIVE

HOW DO YOU FEEL?

It's impossible to describe all the different feelings you can have days, weeks, months, or even years after you learn that your parents are going to split up. Shock, anger, sadness, fear, and depression are just a few of the powerful emotions that teenagers have said they experienced. The strength of each feeling will depend on a lot of things, particularly how your parents broke the news to you, how much conflict there is at home, and what sort of custody arrangements are made.

Shock

"At first I was in shock. I couldn't talk, I couldn't think. I just felt totally dazed."

Jessica (15)

Shock is often the first reaction to a traumatic experience, and it can take many different forms. Like Jessica, some people wander around in a complete daze and become absent-minded, careless, and clumsy.

You may feel like crying or just yelling out loud, and you may not want to speak to anyone.

"I went to my room and put my music on really loud so that no one would hear me, and screamed and screamed."

Jane (15)

Other teenagers had similar reactions.

"I lost it. I started screaming and swearing and crying."
Donna (14)

"I was completely stunned. . . . I couldn't believe that Mom would leave like she did and she wasn't coming back."
Lizzie (18)

"At first, I didn't have any reaction at all. I felt numb. I suppose I was in shock."
Michael (18)

"I remember feeling totally cut off from normal life. I spent most of the time lying in bed, crying."
Natasha (15)

Shock is a perfectly normal, understandable response. These kinds of impulses are your body's natural defense system coming into play—to protect you through this difficult time. However, you can get help with your feelings. Reach out to friends and adults you trust. See your doctor if the physical symptoms are too hard to bear; for instance, if you feel constantly tired and depressed or you can't eat. It may be a good opportunity to talk about what's happened and how you feel about it.

Anger

"When they told me, I felt angry and very unhappy."
Paula (15)

It's very common to feel an explosive anger after the initial shock passes. Many teenagers feel that their parents have let them down and messed up their lives because they've split up. You'll probably be thinking, "How dare they do this!" or, "What about me?" It will all seem very unfair, and you may want to punch or kick something.

Anger can be a particularly difficult emotion to deal with. You might think that showing it will only make the situation worse—that maybe you'll hurt your parents or get them mad at you. As a result, a lot of anger can be swallowed up and never let out.

You need to find an outlet for your anger, but there are good ones and bad ones.

"I felt terrible, I just couldn't cope, and I really rebelled. I skipped school, went out with my friends and got drunk, did a few drugs. Mom went crazy and yelled a lot, but I didn't pay any attention."

Darren (16)

Darren's mom felt helpless. She had a lot of problems maintaining discipline; she felt very guilty about what had happened and consequently let Darren do pretty much as he liked. Darren, for his part, wanted to push his mom as far as he could, just to see how much he could get away with.

"I got arrested for being drunk and disorderly and had to go to court. Luckily, I was let off with a warning because it was my first offense. I won't do that again."

Darren (16)

Using drugs or alcohol to numb the pain is not a good

idea. Neither can provide a permanent solution to your problems, and both just give you a few more to deal with. All they do is temporarily cover up your feelings. When you're sober, those feelings still will be there.

Tess rebelled, too, but in a different way. She felt as if she didn't have a home to go to anymore.

"My parents divorced when I was thirteen. By the time I was sixteen, I was going out practically every night, and when I met Dave, I decided to live with him. I left school and found a job as a secretary."

Tess (20)

Looking back, Tess feels some regret.

"I was far too young, but I felt that I knew best. At sixteen, I wanted my own life. I do regret leaving school. I probably would have gotten a better job if I'd stuck it out, but nobody said anything. My parents seemed so caught up with their own lives, they didn't seem interested. Dave and I are getting married—there doesn't seem anything else to do."

Tess (20)

Like Tess, kids may feel angry and abandoned after a divorce, and sometimes they act without thinking things through. Some teenagers take their anger out on the people closest to them—their friends or the people they live with.

There are more positive ways of dealing with anger. Try some kind of physical exercise, like going for a run or playing a sport. Physical exertion makes you feel more optimistic and better able to cope.

"Every time I felt bad I'd go for a run. It helped a lot.

Plus I got into great shape."

Greg (14)

Pain

"I just cried and cried. I remembered all the good times we'd had and how much things had changed."

Jane (15)

Strong pain and a deep feeling of loss often take the place of anger. These feelings probably will last for a long time, making you feel sad and depressed. The onset of grief is very natural as you begin to mourn the loss of your old life.

Crying really does help. If you can let yourself cry, you can begin to release all those pent-up emotions you are holding inside. And once you can do that, you can begin to deal with things.

Loss

"I got really upset about the whole situation. Dad was horrible to Mom, and I took Mom's side even though I didn't want to take sides. I thought, 'If Dad moves out, it can only get better.' But it hasn't worked out that way. I know what my dad's like, but I wish he was still here."

Jason (16)

Separation and divorce often are compared to death. And

in some ways, the feelings of loss you will experience are very similar. The loss of a parent through divorce can be even more difficult to bear. At least after a death, people generally remember the dead person with affection, and there is none of the bitterness and blaming which are the hallmarks of many split-ups. Death also has a finality about it—you know you won't see the dead person again. If your mom or dad has moved—particularly if he or she just walked out or has moved a long way off—you may have the uncertainty of not really knowing when and if you will see that parent again.

You can have other feelings of loss, too. If you move and change schools, you may lose your friends. You might even feel that you have lost the affection of the parent you live with, particularly if he or she starts to work long hours and has less time to spend with you. The strain of the divorce and lone parenting also makes parents tired and irritable.

These losses may combine to make you feel you no longer have the normal things in life that others take for granted. But there are ways to cope.

"When we moved I felt as if I was losing my whole life. But I kept in touch with my friends, and now I have new friends, too."

Matt (15)

You *can* keep up with friends and family by phone, letter, E-mail, and visits. You can have a close relationship with both parents.

Rejection

"I remember my one concern being that if my mom didn't live with us, she didn't love me anymore."

Lizzie (18)

Rejection is another common feeling. While you might know, deep down, that the absent parent hasn't deliberately turned his or her back on you, it can still feel that way, especially if a parent has walked out, particularly if it's to live with another partner, and even more so if that partner has children. No matter how much explanation you get, whatever reasons you've been given, you still can't help feeling that your parent has abandoned you.

"Dad went to live with Sarah and her two children. I wasn't getting on that well with Mom, and I wanted to go and live with him, but he said it would be really difficult. He'd rejected Mom, and then I really felt he was rejecting me."

Jade (18)

Try to share your feelings with your parent, and give your relationship some time.

Fear

"I felt scared. I thought, 'What's going to happen. . . ? Where am I going to live. . . ? Can I still see my dad?'"

Jessica (15)

Change can be a major source of stress. It's really easy to feel scared and vulnerable if you know there are going to be changes but no one has talked to you about them. There can be big issues and small ones.

Jane and her younger sister, Anita, live in the country, miles away from their school, and have to travel there by car.

"We talked about it all the time. 'If Dad's not here anymore, who's going to drive us to school in the morning?'"

Jane (15)

Lots of questions arise when parents split up, and as a teenager you might find yourself having to ask them. Many parents will not have thought about all the small ways your life will be affected.

Denial

"I thought, if I wait long enough, Mom and Dad will get back together and it will be like it was before. That's what I wanted."

Paula (15)

It's very common for kids to deny that a separation is really happening. Many teenagers try to persuade themselves that the situation is only temporary and that sooner or later their parents will get back together—particularly if parents have a second try at their relationship before they finally break up, or if parents have made a real effort to have a smooth split and still get along well together.

"I tried really hard. When we went out on my birthday, I kept pointing out to Dad how great Mom looked. Like, she'd lost all this weight and wore this really nice dress, not her old jeans like she usually does. I said, 'Go on, Dad, give her a kiss,' but he wouldn't. He looked really embarrassed."

Paula (15)

It took a while before Paula stopped hoping for a "happy ending." Divorce or separation isn't usually a spur of the moment thing. Your parents have probably reached their decision after a lot of thought and painful consideration. Hard as it is, it's more realistic for you to accept the breakup as permanent and begin to get used to it. Then you'll start to feel better. Much later on, you'll recognize you've come through it, and most important of all, you can get on with your own life.

Relief

Sometimes divorce comes as a relief, particularly if your parents constantly fought or one of them drank, or was abusive.

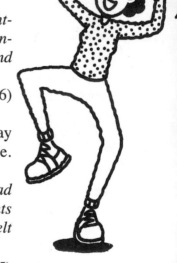

"My mom and dad were always fighting. It was my dad, mostly. To be honest, I just wanted him to go away and leave us alone. I hated him."

Stephen (16)

Conflict creates tension. You may find a separation is best for everyone.

"I didn't realize how the arguing had been getting to me until my parents split up and it stopped. Suddenly I felt much more relaxed."

Matt (15)

One of the ways to cope with the powerful, painful feelings that follow divorce is to understand that they are natural. Divorce hurts. Remember, you will feel better in time.

SIX

PRACTICAL CHANGES

A Parent Moves Out

As soon as your parents have made the decision to split up, or at least to separate for a while, one of them will almost certainly move out and establish a "second home."

"My mom moved out, and I think I miss her more than my brother does. Dad doesn't talk about clothes or boyfriends or other girl stuff. It makes me wish my mom was around more."
Kate (12)

It's hard to actually *believe* a split is happening until a parent leaves home, so that is bound to make you feel sad. Give yourself time and space to think about how you can maintain contact with the parent who has left. Can you talk on the telephone every day? What sort of visits can you arrange? Don't believe you are making a favorite of one parent or being disloyal to the other. Continued contact with both parents will, in most cases, make you feel happier and more confident.

You Move

You may find that you

have to make major changes yourself, such as moving into a new house or starting at a new school.

"I decided who I wanted to live with. I only moved six miles away from my dad, and I had to change schools anyway, so I went to the same one I would have gone to if they hadn't split up. But it was difficult living in a different house, as it was a lot smaller."

Louise (16)

"I was very upset and incredibly excited. I knew we had moved to the city to be near my dad's family because he needed them for support."

Michael (18)

You have to allow for a period of adjustment. Finding your way around and making new friends take time. The change can even be a welcome distraction.

"I had so much new stuff to deal with that I couldn't just dwell on my mom and dad's divorce—I had to move on."

Jade (18)

Two Homes

"After my mom got her own apartment, I started spending two nights a week there. It felt weird at first, but I brought some stuff over—photos, CD's, books—and after a while it was like I had two homes."

Joyce (14)

Even if you don't actually move, once a parent has settled into a new place, you'll probably find yourself spending chunks of time there. Talk to your parent about what you can do to create your own space. Remember, too, you'll need to be extra-organized so you'll have what you need wherever you are.

Having Less Money

"Dad said money was tight, and he had to cut my allowance. I was really angry."

Freddie (16)

Money worries can magnify at this time. It's always more expensive to run two homes than one. Frequently there will be less money available, and if there's a choice between the gas bill and new clothes and entertainment, you can guess which has to win!

"I don't think Mom earns very much, so I work in a shop on weekends so that I can afford to buy clothes and go out."

Rachel (16)

Lack of money can be particularly hard on you if, for example, your friends have more new clothes than you, but it's not the end of the world. Try to find ways of cutting down on spending. You can always earn some money yourself, like Rachel. Even if you're younger than sixteen, jobs like baby-sitting or delivering newspapers are available.

Helping Out

Because of money issues, a parent may have to find a new job or work longer hours. As a result, you can find yourself having to help out more at home.

"Before the divorce, Mom didn't work and she'd put dinner on the table for us. Now that she has a job, she's always tired.

*She just comes in from work and collapses in front of the TV.
I cook dinner and clean up."*

Peter (13)

Nevertheless, you shouldn't
have to keep the household going.
If you feel your parent is being
unreasonable, let him/her know.
You and your parent
will feel better if you
both are clear about
what is expected. Is it
really serious if your
bedroom is a mess?
Isn't it more important
to cook dinner?

*"At first I felt sorry for myself, doing more chores at home,
plus holding down a part-time job. Then I realized I was han-
dling everything and I felt great."*

Gaby (17)

SEVEN

YOU AND YOUR PARENTS

"When Dad left, Mom used to cry all the time. She changed. I couldn't talk to her, she just didn't seem interested, so I just used to shut myself in my room and play my music really loud."

Carla (14)

Understanding What They're Going Through

You can probably understand what your parents are going through, at least partly. It's like splitting up with a boyfriend or girlfriend, but a million times worse. Most couples marry or live together thinking that it's going to be forever, so when the unbelievable happens, they are devastated.

How difficult the split is depends a lot on the circumstances. If one parent just walked out with no prior warning, or if the split was particularly nasty, then it will be extremely hard. If a couple has taken a long time to reach their decision and it's mutual, then it can be less painful. But no matter what, when divorce becomes a reality, feelings like sadness, fear, and guilt surface.

Mom had no warning at all
"Dad walked in and casually announced that he'd met someone else and was leaving. Mom was in shock—he'd given her no warning at all. They'd been together since they were sixteen—my age...."

Rachel (16)

39

Dad fell apart

If your mom or dad has been left for someone else, he or she will feel very hurt, lonely, and rejected. The parent who left will probably feel extremely guilty. Matt's parents separated, and his mom moved out. For the first few months, his dad was really depressed.

"He slept most of the time. He lost all his confidence and interest in life. I was feeling terrible myself, and he wasn't there for me. Finally I talked to him about everything and he snapped out of it."

Matt (15)

Matt's dad was so crushed by the situation that he didn't have enough energy to see to Matt's needs. Just when Matt most needed his help, he was unable to give him support. Fortunately Matt was able to talk to his father and things improved. His dad started to get used to his new life.

Mom misses him

It is very different having to cope on your own when you are used to having another person around, however badly you got along.

"I wish Mom didn't keep watching the phone. She pretends she doesn't, but I know the feeling. She wants him to call and say he's coming back. He's married again, but she's still waiting...."

Jade (18)

Dad said he felt guilty

Parents will feel very guilty, not just about the end of the relationship and the mess they feel they are in, but because they are afraid of what the divorce may have done to you.

"I thought Dad had what he wanted. Sarah's okay and she's quite pretty. Mom's great, but she's let herself go. When Dad told me the other night how guilty he felt, I was really surprised."

Jade (18)

He's lost loads of friends

Splitting up with a partner means much more than losing that person. Friends may side with one parent or the other, especially old friends, who will probably side with the one they knew first, even though they might have been close to the other parent. Relatives in particular may side with one parent.

It's also very hard because couples tend to know other couples and socialize in couples. A single man or woman can suddenly find that his or her social life has gone.

Mom went crazy

If you understand how bad your parents will be feeling, you'll be able to understand if, for instance, they start acting strange or become distant or irritable. Sometimes the change is radical.

"My parents split up a year ago. Mom went crazy for a while. She lost a lot of weight, dyed her hair, and started drinking and doing drugs."

Paula (15)

Supporting a Parent

"When my mom discovered Dad was having an affair, she

freaked. She couldn't cope. She didn't go to work for a week, and was really miserable. I wanted to help, but I mean, what could I do? I had my own problems to deal with. I wanted her to help me."

Jason (16)

It can feel weird when your parents seem to need your help. You're probably used to your parents being there to help you, and suddenly the roles are reversed.

Mom always turned to me
Some parents will use their teenage children for emotional support. Jane's mom found it difficult to cope after her husband left.

"Mom leaned on me. She's always confided in me, and she told me how she felt. Sometimes I felt like I was the grown-up and she was the child."

Jane (15)

"I used to find Mom really embarrassing, but since the divorce we've gotten really close to each other. She's more like a sister than my mom."

Rachel (16)

Try to be sympathetic and understand how painful life can be for someone who is ending a marriage. If, for example, one parent complains about the other to you even though they know it's wrong, or talks obsessively about past history, realize that parent is only giving way to feelings of hurt, anger, and rejection. It's hard for your parent to come to terms with the loss of someone he or she once loved very much.

Remember, though, your first responsibility is to yourself.

If a parent needs more support than you feel you can give, there are organizations that can help. Some are listed at the back of the book.

I gave Mom a break

It's easy to help your mom or dad with the practical things. While you shouldn't have to run the whole household, you can do your part.

"I offered to baby-sit for my little sister once a week for free so Mom could go out and have a break."

Jade (18)

"My mom was in a really bad way, so I'd do the cooking and help with the housework, and a friend of my mom's helped out. It made me realize what a lot she'd done before."

Rachel (16)

Some people adapt to change more quickly than others. Eventually things will become easier, but it does require time and patience.

Caught in the Middle

Divorce is particularly hard if you're being used as a weapon in the battle between parents. But if the divorce has been very nasty, it's tempting for parents to do just that. They might blame each other to you continually; they might use you as a messenger; they can force you to choose between them; one parent can be deliberately difficult about visits, either by never being at the right place at the right time or by finding reasons to change plans. Here are a few teenagers' experiences.

I felt like I was being pulled apart

"My mom hated me talking about my dad. It was like he didn't exist, so I kept talking about him, and she thought I was just annoying her on purpose. I mean, I love my dad. It really upset me."

Jane (15)

"My parents still fight about everything. They say really mean things to each other, and then my mom cries. I can't stand it. I yell at them to stop, but all they do is tell me to butt out. I don't know what to do."

Darren (16)

During a breakup, parents can get so caught up in their own feelings that they forget yours.

They involved me in their fights

John was thirteen when his parents divorced. Both of them decided that John ought to live with them and embarked on a long, bitter fight for custody. There were constant battles.

"It was awful. Every time they had a fight, they'd try and get me involved. Dad said he'd never agree to me living with Mom. Mom said he was a drunk and that no way was he taking me down to the club every night when he went drinking. Dad said all she cared about was her new boyfriend. He made me say I wanted to live with him, but when the social worker asked me where I wanted to go, I just broke down and wouldn't say. I didn't know where I wanted to go, I just wanted someone to tell me where. I felt bad. Mom has this big family, but my dad hasn't got anyone. He's just got me, and I feel really sorry for him. Yeah, my dad drinks, he can be pretty awful, but I can talk to him about things. Football. Mom isn't interested. It wasn't right. I was really fed up with the way they played me off against each other."

John (16)

Dad asked me to spy on Mom

"Every time I see my dad, he asks me what Mom's up to, if she's seeing anyone, stuff like that. Why doesn't he ask her instead of trying to get me to spy on her?"

Chris (15)

They got jealous over me

Donna's parents used her as a weapon.

"Sometimes, well, they'd both fight about me, or get jealous over me. They both said they wanted me to live with them, but I wanted to live with my grandma. I kept telling them it was none of my business and to work it out themselves, but they didn't listen."

Donna (14)

Dealing with Conflict

Your parents have no right to try to make you take sides. The best thing for you to do is to tell them that you love them both and you're not going to choose one of them over the other. If one parent asks you to spy on the other, tell him that if he wants to know something, he'll have to find out for himself. Neither of your parents is owed more loyalty than the other. Never get involved in their arguments. Simply walk away. There's no point talking to them until they've stopped fighting.

If the constant fights get you down, wait until things get calmer and tell them that all the arguments and bickering are really painful and upsetting for you. They may not even be aware of how you feel. Once they are, they might begin to understand what they are doing to themselves and to you.

If you find talking to them difficult, why not write a letter? Writing things down is a good strategy for other reasons, too—it can help you organize your thoughts and feelings, and while it won't solve the problems, it may make you feel better.

Trying Not to Blame

"I blame my mom. She's the one that had an affair in the first place. Then my dad went off and had an affair to get back at her."

Jessica (15)

Jessica felt very angry that her mom had an affair, and, as she saw it, was therefore responsible for the family breakdown. However, when she and her mom sat down and talked, Jessica got her mother's side of the story. Jessica's mom told her that she had felt very frustrated and lonely because her dad was a "workaholic" and stayed late at the office every night and on weekends.

It might seem obvious to you that one parent is to blame—if, for instance, like Jessica, your mom had an affair first, your dad's an alcoholic, or one parent has walked out on the other.

Always remember there are things you don't know and there are two sides to every situation.

Living with One Parent

Living with one parent instead of two is a big change. Usually, the parents decide where the children will live, and sometimes they ask for their children's opinions. If parents can't agree, a judge will make the decision, probably after talking with you about what you want. (See pages 86-90 for more information on divorce law.) Deciding which parent to live with is a terrible decision to have to make, particularly if you just want to be with them both. Choosing who to live with is not choosing who you love most. The answer is for you to work out where you would feel happiest and most secure and to let your parents know.

Freddie didn't want to live with his mom.

"We were always arguing. She didn't like my friends coming over, and she was totally unreasonable about what time I came in at night. I said I wanted to live with my dad—and I did."
Freddie (16)

"It was obvious I was going to live with my mom because my dad's a singer and was often on tour and so I was used to having Mom around. Now Dad lives in another country, so I go for vacations and alternate Christmasses."
Jessica (15)

In practice, it's still more common for children to stay

with their moms, the usual argument being that mothers are more used to looking after kids. Of course, many fathers are just as good at parenting, and many children do live very happily with their dads.

All kinds of living arrangements are possible. Some children live with one parent most of the time, and see the other parent on a regular schedule, perhaps on weekends. Some live first with one and then the other on a short- or long-term basis. For instance, if parents live far away from each other, kids may spend the school year with one parent, the summer with the other. Your family will try to come up with a plan that works for everyone.

Whoever you live with, you will miss the other parent, and that parent will miss you. Remember that just because one parent is not living with you, he or she is still your parent. It may not be so easy for parents to show how much they care, particularly if they are living miles away and see their kids only on vacations or holidays, but it's possible to get over a lot of the difficulties by talking and taking the opportunity to show care and concern. However hard it is, it's usually worth maintaining contact if you can, even by letter or telephone.

I see my dad on weekends

"Every weekend either my sister, myself, or both of us stays Friday or Saturday night at my dad's house. He sometimes visits during the week. It's good because I still see my dad."

Louise (16)

It's up to me to make arrangements

"I see my dad once a week. It's up to me to make arrangements."

Paula (15)

"I lived with my mom for a while before I saw my dad regularly. That really upset me, so I talked to Mom about it. Now I see Dad whenever I want to, mostly at weekends."

Jane (15)

Problem Parents

Sometimes a parent can have problems that get in the way of having a relationship with you.

It might be dangerous to see my dad

"My mom didn't want us to see my dad because he was dealing drugs and she didn't want me to be caught up in the drugs. And I don't want to see him; I think he's rotten for not helping my mom."

Rachel (16)

This can be hard to accept, but it might be dangerous for you to see one parent. Perhaps your parent is very violent or is a drug addict. Obviously you should listen to what people say, but if you really miss your parent, you might ask if the separation means that all contact has to be broken. Perhaps you still could phone or write to keep the relationship going.

He can't be bothered to see me

It can be very painful if you lose contact with one of your parents, if, for example, he or she has moved out and has decided not to keep in touch. The important thing to remember is that you aren't to blame. Your parent may have problems, but that doesn't mean there is something wrong with you.

"At first my mom would call or write once in a while. Then I

stopped hearing from her altogether. It hurt a lot. But slowly
I realized it wasn't me—she was really messed up."

Tania (14)

"Since the split, I think Dad hates me, because he ignores me.
He's not interested in anything I do, or what I've got to say."

Rachel (16)

If you feel sure a parent doesn't want to see you, all you can do is accept it and move on. But remember, things may not necessarily be as they seem. For instance, if your mom's the "guilty party"—say, she left your dad for another man—she may feel very bad and think that you won't want to see her. Make sure your parents know that you want to keep in touch with both of them. Even if your parents are at loggerheads, you can make your own arrangements to see each of them. And don't feel as if you're betraying the parent you're living with—it's only natural to want to see both your parents, whatever happened.

I don't want to see my dad
"My mom knew that I would never want to live with my dad.
I don't want to see him, but my sister sees him."

Rachel (16)

Even if you don't want to see the absent parent now, you might change your mind in the future. Leave your options open—write or phone instead.

Dividing Your Time: Issues

My parents have totally different rules
"My dad won't let us have candy or gum or watch TV sitcoms

or stay out on school nights. My mom's fine about that stuff, but she's psycho about cleaning up. My dad is mega-messy. Actually though, it's cool to have such a total change."

Vanessa (14)

Lots of parents have different do's and don'ts. If you find it tough to adjust, talk to both parents.

I always feel upset when I visit Mom

It can be hard having two homes, especially to start. If visiting your parent is painful or upsetting, then you should discuss the situation with both parents or ask a third party to intervene. No one should be forced to visit if he or she doesn't want to.

Think about it, though. Is the upsetting thing having to leave?

"I love seeing Mom, but almost every time I leave, I feel like crying."

Julie (14)

Going home again after seeing the absent parent can make you feel sad, but holding on to the fact that you will be seeing your mom or dad again soon, and making plans, can help.

I want to be with my friends

As you get older, it's natural to want to spend more time with people your own age. You should be able to schedule your visits yourself to take account of your needs and your social life, rather than being bound by the lifestyle of your parent. Taking care of yourself doesn't make you disloyal.

Chris found that it was a problem pleasing both his father and himself. He felt really guilty because he was bored when he was with his dad.

"I spend every weekend with my dad. We really get along, and I know he enjoys my visits. The trouble is, I end up feeling really bored. Dad makes me feel guilty because on a Saturday night I want to go out with my friends, not sit at home and watch TV, no matter how much he likes having me around."

Chris (15)

Even if you feel guilty, you must think of yourself, too. As a teenager you are beginning to be independent of your parents and to form close relationships outside your family. Making the break from a single parent can be particularly difficult. Chris's dad felt lonely and wanted his son's company. Luckily, Chris himself didn't feel under too much pressure, and he spoke to his dad and said that he would be out with his friends on Saturday. His dad was disappointed at first, but he soon got used to it, and on Sunday, Chris was much better company.

I can talk to my dad now

There may be unexpected benefits to having two homes.

"Before the divorce, I didn't feel close to my dad. It was really difficult to have a normal relationship with him because he was always putting down my mom. I feel pretty happy now, and I don't feel I've missed out by not having him around all the time. I've discovered that when I do see him I can talk to him about most things. I even told him when I started my period, and he was really cool about it."

Jane (15)

EIGHT

FACING THE WORLD

What Will Your Friends Think?

"I didn't want to tell anybody at first. I was really embarrassed. But of course, it was dumb, because lots of people at school have divorced parents."

Louise (16)

When the split happens you will find that you have to deal not only with your emotions and practical changes, but also with the attitudes of people outside the immediate family. You may be nervous about breaking the news, and it may take a while before you feel ready.

"I didn't tell anyone for a long time. Not even my best friend, and she has always been there for me. I just couldn't. I used to sit away from my friends at school and think about what it would be like if my mom and dad were still together. Once, when my friends asked me what was wrong, I just said nothing and tried to shake it off. Then one day I just came straight out with it. My friends were nice and they didn't make a big deal about it but made sure I was okay."

Louise (16)

It's natural to feel embarrassed and uncomfortable if one parent leaves. However, most people will understand, since divorce is so common these days. According to statistics, about half of all marriages don't work out.

It's a good idea to tell your friends what's going on, however hard it is. Hiding the truth can get really complicated. Friends can be very supportive, and some may well have been through similar experiences themselves.

"I only told my friends who were really close. My best friend was very understanding. She's been through it herself, and I felt much better telling someone who knew what I was talking about."

Jane (15)

"I was really casual. Some friends asked why I was moving, and I brought it up then."

Michael (18)

Telling Other People

"Talk to my teacher? No way!"

Paula (15)

Do your teachers know about the split? Your parents will probably tell your teachers, but you might think seriously about talking to them too, particularly if you feel that you're working less hard or doing less well than usual. Teachers will be sympathetic if they know what's going on at home.

"I felt pretty depressed. I didn't bother with my homework, and of course, my grades went down. My teacher asked me what was up. I thought he was going to be really nasty, but I told him my parents had just split up, and we got talking

about it. I felt much better after that. He was really nice."

Tony (16)

Nothing to Hide

"After the divorce I moved to a new house and changed schools. I was totally miserable and I didn't tell anyone at first that my parents were divorced. If anyone asked me if anything was wrong, I said no. After I discovered other people in my class had parents who were divorced, I felt better."

Paula (15)

"I was worried people would think differently of me if they knew, so I avoided their questions. Then I decided that it was best to be up front—just give straight answers. Nobody mentioned it after that, and I realized it wasn't a big deal."

John (16)

Some teenagers cover up their feelings because they are frightened of what people might think, but as Paula and John found out, telling everyone is usually a relief.

Quiz: How Do You Handle Your Emotions?

When you come up against a difficult situation, how do you react? Do you hit the roof, do you try to be levelheaded and reasonable about it, or do you brood quietly, keeping your feelings secret?

1. Your boyfriend/girlfriend cheats on you with your best friend. You:
a) tell him/her where to get off.
b) have a quiet cry about it, then try to put it down to experience.
c) say nothing but get really depressed.

2. Your pet dies. You:

a) hold a funeral service.

b) make a decision to get another one as soon as possible.

c) just put it out of your mind.

3. Your boyfriend/girlfriend tells you that his/her ex is constantly calling up just to talk. You:

a) tell your boyfriend/girlfriend that he/she should tell the ex to get lost.

b) tell yourself you're not the jealous type and you trust him/her completely.

c) say nothing and continue to smile sweetly.

4. You're unavoidably late meeting a friend and he/she gets mad at you. You:

a) storm off in a huff and spend the evening in front of the TV.

b) ask him/her to calm down and explain why you're late.

c) say nothing but spend the night feeling guilty.

5. You've had a lot of late nights—you're feeling wiped out. A friend calls you and asks you to a party. You:

a) go along but make it clear over and over again that you're doing him/her a big favor.

b) explain that you're having an early night and take a rain check.

c) go along and try to enjoy yourself, hating every minute.

6. At a party, you see someone you'd like to meet.

When you catch his/her eye, you:
a) flirt outrageously and draw as much attention to yourself as you can.
b) smile.
c) look the other way.

7. You've seen these terrific must-have sneakers but your allowance won't cover the cost. You:
a) have a major tantrum and demand that your parent gives you the extra money.
b) make up your mind to take that Saturday job and pay for them yourself.
c) go to your room and sulk.

How did you score?

Mostly A's: You don't believe in hiding your emotions, and you are quick to let people know exactly how you feel. But be careful. Going over the top isn't necessarily the way to get what you want. You're not the only one with feelings.

Mostly B's: You're Mr./Ms. Cool. You don't indulge in tantrums, and you've got the good sense to solve your problems practically. Just one thing: Be sure you're not scared to get angry. After all, pretty much everybody blows up once in a while.

Mostly C's: People probably find you well-adjusted and easygoing. Really, though, you are someone who has trouble letting anyone know how you feel. This is dangerous. Denying your feelings is depriving you of many things, maybe even the ability to enjoy your life.

NINE

SINGLE PARENTS

"Everything changed. We didn't have much money, so we moved to an apartment and Mom had to get a job. She never worked when we were small, but now that she's got her career going again, I can see that she's a lot happier because she's more free and individual and able to do her own thing."

Paula (15)

When your parents split up, it's likely that one, or both, will be single for the first time in quite a few years. Some parents settle very happily into their single state, but others can take a bit longer to adjust.

Is This My Mother?

"My mom colored her hair and started taking tennis lessons. I didn't even know she liked tennis."

Matt (15)

It's very common for the newly divorced or separated to act young again, particularly if they've spent months, or even years, trapped in unhappy relationships. Imagine the feeling—freedom. Your parents are finally divorced, and now they can get on with their lives. They might make some changes, but don't worry—underneath, they're the same people.

Parents Dating

"Mom seems to go out almost every night. I don't like it."

Jessica (15)

"How could she get involved with someone so soon after the divorce? I hate her boyfriend. He's a creep. I'm doing everything I can to make him go away."

Carla (14)

Ruining your parent's relationship, like Carla is trying to do, is not a good idea. How would you feel if your parents told you that you couldn't date?

From your point of view it's probably very difficult to think of your parents ever dating, so when they do start, it doesn't seem right.

Dating can even seem like a betrayal. Things have just happened too fast. That may be true, but if you can, think about it from your parent's point of view.

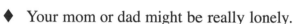

♦ Your mom or dad might be really lonely.

♦ They might miss having sex (which is probably hard for you to think about).

♦ They haven't gotten used to being single, and want to find new partners with whom to start relationships.

♦ They feel worthless, especially if they were left for someone else. They need to feel attractive again.

"I don't think Mom liked herself very much. Dad was always putting her down, and she believed it. All those men she

dated, I think she was trying to prove she was still attractive or something."

Olivia (15)

It's very common for a newly single parent to see many different people. However, your parent isn't going to have multiple partners forever. Sooner or later most people settle down into one special relationship.

Lizzie's parents split up when she was fourteen, and she lived with her dad. At first he dated a lot.

"I didn't like it. I'd come in and find Dad kissing somebody on the sofa. But I never said anything, I just accepted it. I felt very relieved when he met Caroline. They've been together for three years now, and seem very happy."

Lizzie (18)

Gay Parents

You might not know one of them is gay until your parents split up and start dating again.

"When Dad told me he was gay, it didn't make me feel any different about him; I just accepted it."

Jamie (15)

Very few gay parents are awarded custody of children even when there is evidence of good parenting and a close relationship between parent and child. Unfortunately, society still holds a prejudiced view of the same-sex family, though this is slowly changing. The truth is that a gay family can be as loving and caring as a heterosexual one.

Jamie's parents separated when he was thirteen and his dad moved in with his partner.

"I live with my mom, but I spend weekends with my dad and his partner. I get on really well with both my parents. I don't think there are any differences between ourselves and other families."

Jamie (15)

It is probably wise to take care whom you tell. Don't leave yourself open to teasing or bullying from ignorant people.

"We decided to keep it quiet in case Dad was gay-bashed. My big worry was that I would lose my friends if they knew. I've told my friends now. Most are fine, but others try to get me worked up. The teachers at school are supportive. My advice to kids who are getting hassled because one of their parents is gay is to ignore it. It doesn't change the way your parents feel about you. They still love you."

Jamie (15)

Parents' New Relationships

"At first, Mom's boyfriends were like clones of my dad. That was okay as far as I'm concerned. It was more difficult for me when she took up with some guy who was a real dork. She still sees him sometimes."

Olivia (15)

The chances are that at some point your parents will have new partners. Try not to compare them with your other parent, however hard that might be. Don't automatically hate them, even if your dad or mom's new partner was partly responsible for the breakup.

You probably love your parents no matter what they have done, and it's easier all around if you try to get along with the people they've chosen to be with. If you're against the new relationship, ask yourself why. Are you worried that if your parent falls in love, he/she will love you less? Are you afraid that your parent might remarry and have a new family? Once you've acknowledged your fears, then you can deal with them.

Sometimes, though, you just won't like a particular person no matter how hard you try. It happens. On the other hand, sometimes a parent will be with a person you're happy to have in your life.

"I love my mom, but Barbara is awesome. She takes me sailing, and she's great to talk to."

Nicole (14)

Remember, your opinion had no affect on your parents' decision to divorce, and your opinion will have little affect on your parents' new relationships. Try to make the best of it. You have a life to live, and it isn't worth hassling everyone else about decisions you can't change.

Your parent might even decide to make the new relationship permanent....

TEN

STEP BY STEP

Stepfamilies can be full-time or part-time, perhaps getting together only on weekends or during school vacations, but every stepfamily is a challenge, particularly at the start.

The most important thing for you to remember is that you, your parent, your stepparent, and your stepsiblings (if you have any) are going to have very strong but mixed feelings over the change. On the one hand, you might be looking forward to the arrival of a new parent, but on the other, you'll probably be reluctant to take on the changes that will inevitably follow. Your parent and stepparent will, of course, be hoping that everything will work out for the best.

How Do You Feel About the Marriage?

"At first I was afraid that my stepdad was going to be a really horrible person. I think it's because I'd heard so many awful things about stepfamilies. You know, kids getting abused by their stepparents and everything."

Stephen (16)

Stephen was scared to be in a stepfamily. It's also very common to feel:

Sad

While neither of your parents is in a permanent relationship, you still can dream that they'll get back together. You can't anymore.

Jealous

Having gone through the trauma of a divorce with your parent, you probably will have developed a close relationship. Not surprisingly, the appearance of a new man or woman can be a shock, and you may feel as if you are being pushed into second place. Jealousy can range from a slight feeling of discomfort to a full-blown sense of bitterness and betrayal.

Angry

"I couldn't believe that Mom liked Mike more than my dad, and I hated him. Whenever he came to the house, I'd give him a hard time. Mom got really annoyed, but I didn't care."

Jessica (15)

You're particularly likely to get angry if you feel that the stepparent is taking the place of the absent parent.

"Then Mike moved in. He treated the place like it was his own. I felt really angry. I'd been through enough without having to get used to some guy around."

Jessica (15)

These feelings all are normal. Acknowledge them and talk about them. You might also feel:

Hopeful

"My dad never had time for us. Like, he'd never come to see me in the school plays. He always had some excuse, work, usually. I really thought my stepdad would be different."

Rachel (16)

You might hope that the new member of the family will

be able to provide you with the things your absent parent wasn't able to give you.

If you hope for too much, you are likely to be disappointed. Remember that your stepparent is only human and can never make up for the bad things that have happened.

Guilty

Maybe you like your stepparent a lot and you worry that your mom or dad would be hurt if they knew.

"Feel your feelings. It's okay to like your parent's new person, and it's okay not to."

Gaby (17)

Stepparents

My mom's being replaced

For many teenagers, being part of a stepfamily is not something to look forward to or enjoy, particularly after a painful divorce. Janet's dad married again soon after he split up with her mom.

"Sharon wasn't my mom, never could be my mom. I think I hurt her a lot, because she wanted to get close and I wouldn't let her. I think if she had been my real mom she'd have been pretty good."

Janet (14)

Janet, who lived with her father, refused to have anything to do with Sharon. Whenever Sharon came over, Janet would disappear into her room and stay there. The situation got worse when Sharon moved in.

"I felt I'd already been through a lot of changes, and now I was expected to accept this person living in our house. I didn't want another mom."

Janet (14)

Janet felt that her mom was being replaced, which was untrue. It's important to remember that just because you have another family, it doesn't mean the old one doesn't exist anymore. Your parents will always be your parents. A stepmom or stepdad doesn't replace your real mom or dad. You don't have to like them or love them, but you should try to get along with them.

My stepmother doesn't like me
"I sort of get along with her, but it's hard because she doesn't seem to care if I'm there or not."

Kate (12)

You've probably grown up with fairy tales featuring "wicked stepmothers." Remember Hansel and Gretel, whose stepmother hated them and plotted to get rid of them? Or Cinderella? The reality is that stepparents are not monsters. They want, if possible, to have a good relationship with you.

Think about it from their point of view. Stepparenting can be tough—especially when teenagers are involved. It's as new to them as it is to you, and stepparents are probably very anxious about how they are going to cope, particularly if they feel you resent them being there and everything they do is wrong. They need all the friends they can get. Adjusting to the changes will be difficult at first, but with a little bit of time and effort, you might discover that your stepparents aren't so bad after all. You might even get to like them.

My stepdad's so strict

"We moved in with my stepdad and his two kids. He had about a million rules he wanted me to follow. (No phone calls on school nights!) My mom and I got him to lighten up."

Greg (14)

There will be lots of changes, and it may not be easy. Gradually, your stepfamily and you will begin to adopt new rules to suit the new setup, for example, on TV watching, staying out late, homework, etc. Everyone needs to agree on what these rules are and what happens if they are broken. There will have to be give and take on both sides. Sure, from your point of view, stepparents don't have the same rights as parents, but there are bound to be times when a stepparent feels that he or she has to lay down the law. The only way to sort out problems is to talk about them. If you feel, for example, that some of the new rules are unfair, then discuss them with your parent and stepparent and work out a mutually acceptable solution.

If you feel your natural parent is the only one who can lay down the rules, then you should discuss this rather than have an argument with your stepparent.

Dad's so different now

"When Dad married Claire, he really changed."

Kate (12)

A stepparent can bring out sides of your parent's personality you've never seen before. Different people do that—think how you change depending on who you're with. Still, it can be unsettling and it takes some getting used to. If you can, spend some time alone with your parent to discuss how he or she has changed and how it makes you feel.

Of course, you might even find that a new relationship improves a parent.

"My dad was really messy. He left his dirty clothes on the floor and his muddy shoes in the kitchen. Yuk! My mom always put up with it, but my stepmom—she made him pick his own stuff up and clean his own shoes."

Mark (15)

Now that I know her better, she's okay

"I hated my stepmom, Sharon, but now that I know her better, I think she's really sweet and nice. There are some things we disagree on, and she aggravates me a lot, but she's okay really."

Janet (14)

Teenagers who get along with their stepparents best agree that they are like good friends, people who can give them help or advice, provide a shoulder to cry on, and perhaps even share hobbies and interests. As a friend, a stepparent may criticize and give advice but doesn't assume the authority of a parent.

Stepsiblings

Did your stepmom or stepdad come complete with kids? Accepting a stepbrother or sister can be very hard.

My stepsister's boring

"I felt really angry when Mom told us Steph, my stepsister, was coming to live here. I found it hard at first. Steph wouldn't talk

to anyone and was really boring."

Donna (14)

It took some time and effort, but eventually Donna discovered that because both of them had been through a hard time when their parents divorced, she and her stepsister actually had something in common. They became good friends. Not that there weren't problems to overcome. When her mom remarried, Donna had to share a room with her stepsister. She didn't like it, but she tried hard to accept it.

I have a crush on my stepbrother
"My stepbrother was absolutely gorgeous. Not like his dad, who's a complete nerd."

Jade (18)

It's quite common for teenagers in stepfamilies to find themselves attracted to one another. Although they're not illegal, these relationships are very difficult. It's best to avoid them if you can. At your age, you're probably not looking for a permanent relationship, you're still experimenting. Remember that when the romance ends, you're still going to be stepsiblings.

My mom spoils my stepsister
"My stepsister's always using my makeup or borrowing my clothes, and it really makes me angry. I told my mom, but she didn't think it was a big deal. I wish she wouldn't always take my stepsister's side."

Donna (14)

You might find that your mom or dad bends over backwards to try to be fair to a stepchild and not favor you.

Donna's case is typical. Donna felt that her mom had taken her stepsister's side and that she cared more about her stepsister. In fact, Donna's mom was so anxious to get along with her stepdaughter that she tended to be hard on her own child. Once she realized how Donna felt, she was able to talk to her stepdaughter and tell her to ask Donna first before she borrowed anything.

"When I visited Dad, it was fun having a stepbrother to do things with, but my father wasn't there for me. He showed favoritism to my stepbrother. He spent more time with him than me. I really felt pushed into the background."

Jason (16)

I like being part of a big family
You may be surprised how well it can all work out.

"I was an only child before, but my stepfather has two kids of his own. At first it was weird, but now I like being a member of a big family, even if one of them is a complete dork."

Tina (15)

. . . and A Baby

It brought me and my stepbrothers together
"I was upset when Mom told us she was pregnant. So were my stepbrothers. None of us liked it. It was the first time we had agreed on anything. We were pretty mean to Mom during her pregnancy."

Rachel (16)

As Rachel and her stepbrothers saw it, her mother and stepfather were creating a third family, to which none of them would belong. They felt pushed out and bound up together in mutual hate of the situation. They worried that their parents wouldn't love them as much as the new baby.

"Amazingly, when Pete was born, it brought us together because we felt he belonged to both families."

Rachel (16)

"I think it's nice. I enjoy being second eldest, and I consider my half brothers and sisters as my real brothers and sisters and would never treat them below my real brother because they are just as important to me. Best of all is that my half brothers and sisters and my stepmom can give me relief and a different type of relationship than I get with my real family."

Louise (16)

Surviving Your Stepfamily: Tips

♦ Be tolerant.

♦ Remember, you don't have to love your step-family.

♦ Be kind.

♦ Try to obey the family rules.

♦ Remember that it's just as tough for them as it is for you.

♦ Be honest about how you feel. Don't bottle up angry or resentful feelings. If something bothers you, talk about it and try to work it out.

♦ Don't be too hard on yourself. Remember that it's going to take time to get used to the changes.

♦ Have a sense of humor.

ELEVEN

I WILL SURVIVE

While you are going through a family breakup, you may feel as if your whole world has shattered and things will never be the same again. Everyone's emotions are in chaos; nobody knows what to do. You may wonder how you'll get through it.

Well, you will. Most people are survivors, and tough experiences are part of life. As we struggle with them, we grow as people and learn to deal better with whatever happens. You will probably find that you've gained something positive from the experience. Many teens think that living through a family divorce has made them more mature and independent at younger ages.

It's Not All Bad!

"My sister and I never really talked much. She's a couple of years younger than me. . . and I thought she was a real baby. When Mom and Dad split up, she was the only person who understood me, and we really got to know each other. She's my best friend now."

Jade (18)

"I actually enjoy seeing my parents separately. I spend

more time with them now, and they make a real effort to do things, like taking me to places that I like."

Louise (16)

"I've become far more grown up in a lot of ways because I've had to solve a lot of problems, which might not have happened if they hadn't divorced."

Janet (14)

"In many ways I see my mom as a person who I really like, and talk to. Before, she was just there."

John (16)

"I was an only child before—and it's great having some stepbrothers around."

Tina (15)

"I have changed. I had to be strong and supportive when they started leaning on me—sharing their problems with me—and it made me grow up a lot."

Jane (15)

"I'm a lot stronger and less naive. I had to be more independent, and I was shown the world as it really is."

Rachel (16)

Helping Yourself

Keep talking
"Talk to someone. It always helps to have someone to lean on."

Lizzie (18)

Talking is probably the most positive way you can help yourself. Talking about a problem nearly always makes you feel better. Hiding it makes you feel worse. Facing your fears, thinking and talking about them, however difficult and upsetting that may be at first, helps you feel more in control of your life. Feelings left unexplored, slowly but surely fester inside and could seriously damage your relationships with those around you. You have to remember, too, that talking about these feelings once or twice won't be enough. The painful feelings that often result from divorce need courage, time, and patience to work through.

Write it down

"I started keeping a journal right after I got the news. I just poured everything out. It saved me."

Joyce (14)

Writing is another great way to help yourself.

You might try:

♦ **A diary** with entries made as often as you like, charting what's going on, how you are feeling, and the changes you are experiencing

♦ **My life story**, an album or scrapbook of your life

Here are a few things you might include:

♦ A family tree, with your half siblings if you have them, and even your stepfamily

♦ Family photos, pictures, letters, and other memorabilia

♦ Special or funny stories

Do what works for you

You may have special things you do that help when you're going through hard times.

"For me it's music. I'd just go to my room, put on my headphones, and listen."

Julie (14)

"I take walks in the woods. All the growing things and the special quiet calm me down."

Brad (15)

People Who Can Help

There are a lot of people you could talk to who can sympathize and give you advice, if you want it.

Your parents

Often when you have problems, parents are the most obvious people to turn to. They love you and want the best for you. But you may need to give them a chance to adjust before they'll really be able to help. At the time of a breakup, many parents find talking difficult.

Family or friends

Sisters or brothers can be a real support—they will understand what you feel because they are going through exactly the same experience. What about your best friend? Other people your own age who have gone through family divorces are great. Knowing that you're not the only one to find yourself in this situation will make you feel less isolated. It also helps to learn that people do recover.

Professionals

Sometimes talking with somebody who doesn't know you or your family intimately can be more valuable than talking to either friends or relatives. The right person could be a teacher at school, a doctor, or a counselor. You'll want somebody who makes you feel safe and comfortable. There are also organizations you can contact, such as those listed at the back of this book.

Don't be afraid to ask for help. You can approach some professionals—a teacher or school guidance counselor, for instance—on your own. Or you may want to ask your parents to help you find a counselor or therapist.

"After seeing a counselor, I could cope with other issues and talk to people more easily."

Jessica (15)

Don't let anyone discourage you from taking care of yourself. This is a time to really examine what you want and what you think you need.

"For once in your life, think about yourself and no one else. Talk to as many people as you can and hold on, because if you do it'll be over before you know it."

Lizzie (18)

"You have to work out what's best for yourself. Tell your parents, and don't let them mess you up."

Freddie (16)

We've Been There

In the questionnaire I prepared to gather information for this book, I asked teenagers what advice they would give a friend who was experiencing the crisis of his or her parents' separation or divorce. Here are some of the answers.

"Talk about it. Don't bottle up your feelings. It's important to be honest about how you feel."

Tess (20)

"Just try and be positive about it."

Paula (15)

"Don't be embarrassed about having divorced parents. It's sad, but it's not the end of the world."

Jessica (15)

"Don't worry about it; it's not your fault, and things will get better soon."

Louise (16)

"Sympathize with your parents and let them do what is best for them and for you."

Jamie (15)

Looking to the Future

Time really does have a way of making things better. You may remember Tess, whose parents divorced when she was thirteen. Seven years later, she is able to look back and put things in perspective.

"If people can't live in harmony and do not see eye to eye, it's best for all concerned for the parents to go their separate ways. It doesn't seem like it at the time, but looking back, it is."

Tess (20)

Many teenagers worry that having seen their parents separate, their own relationships will be doomed to failure. Although there is some evidence to show that the children of divorcees are more likely to go through divorces themselves, that doesn't necessarily mean it's going to happen to you. What's most important is the type of person you are, the kind of family you come from, and the way you relate to the people you love.

Although it is useful to observe a good relationship in action, the opposite is true, too. If you watch your parents make mistakes, you learn what not to do!

A Survival Guide: Tips

♦ Other people have come through family breakups and survived. So will you.

♦ Life isn't perfect. Try to accept that life has its ups and downs.

♦ Bad things will happen, but the good things will help you get over them.

♦ Keep saying to yourself, "This, too, will pass." Time has a way of making things better.

♦ Don't go on a guilt trip. It's not your fault.

♦ Make sure you get as much information as possible so that you know what's going on.

♦ Make decisions that are right for you.

♦ Talk about it.

♦ Ask for what you need.

♦ Be good to yourself.

A Last Word

It can be hard at first, but in time, you and your parents will grow to accept the changes that come with a breakup. Once you've come through it and recovered, you might even find life is better than it was before.

Let Louise have the last word:

"Even though things have been bad, I don't think I've ever regretted my parents' getting divorced. They never could get along. The fights were awful. It's better without all that. Sure, I wish they could have been more friendly, but things turned out different. The best thing to come out of it is that Mom and I are much closer than we used to be. We get along really well. Getting divorced is not the end of the world. It hasn't put me off marriage, but I hope I never have to go through it myself."

Louise (16)

HELP: A SPECIAL SECTION

No matter what your problem, you can find organizations out there that will give you advice and support. They are run by understanding, experienced people who genuinely want to help. There is no charge for calling an 800 number and the call won't show up on your phone bill. Remember that sometimes these numbers are very busy, so if you can't get through at first, keep trying.

"I really wanted to find a support group, but I didn't know how. Finally I went to my guidance counselor and she helped me make some calls. I found a group that was really great. A couple of the people I met there are still good friends of mine."
Sarah (16)

Finding a Counselor or a Support Group

You and your parents can ask your friends, family, doctor, school, church or synagogue, or insurance/health plan for names of support groups or therapists. Even though you might feel uncomfortable about asking around, it will be very helpful if you can find a counselor who is known by someone you trust.

For teen support groups, you can also contact:

♦ *American Self-Help Clearinghouse (973) 625-7101.* Will tell you about local support groups in your area.

♦ *Rainbows (800) 266-3206.* Peer support groups for children (K-12) and adults who have suffered a loss such as a divorce or a death. They will train people in your school, or church/synagogue to run these support groups.

- *GLPCI (Gay and Lesbian Parent Coalition) (202) 583-8029. COLAGE (Children of Lesbian and Gays Everywhere) 3543 18th Street #17, San Francisco, California. (415) 861-5437.*

These two groups, GLPCI and COLAGE, which are connected, make up an international support, educational, and advocacy organization for gay, lesbian, and bi-sexual parents and their families. Services include support groups, a newsletter, internet resources, conferences, trips, and outings.

If you need help locating a licensed therapist in your community, these professional organizations can give you the phone number of your local chapter, which frequently will have a therapist directory for all the major cities in your state. These referrals are for private counselors who charge an hourly fee:

- *American Psychiatric Association (202) 682-6000.*

- *American Psychological Association (800) 964-2000.* They will transfer you to the office nearest you while you are on the phone with them.

- *The Clinical Social Work Federation (800) 270-9739.*

You can also use on-line directories to help you locate a therapist:

- *American Association of Marriage and Family Therapy www.AAMFT.org*

- *American Board of Examiners in Clinical Social Work www.ABECSW.org*

- *American Psychiatric Association www.psych.org* On-line list of branch offices to contact for the names of psychiatrists in your community. Click APA members, then APA District Branches.

Hotlines

If you need to talk to someone right away, try a hotline number. Remember, an 800 number can be called free of charge from anywhere in the United States:

♦ *National Youth Crisis Hotline (800) 448-4663*. General crisis intervention and referral for any teenage issue or problem.

♦ *Covenant House (800) 999-9999*. Counselors are available 24 hours a day. Teen crisis line for any kind of problem, including running away, family violence, and suicidal feelings. Will deliver messages between runaways and their families.

♦ *National Runaway Switchboard (800) 621-4000*. 24-hour-a-day crisis hotline for runaway youth. Message service for kids and parents. Provides help with options and developing a plan of action. Will tell you about local resources in your city.

♦ *Suicide Prevention (310) 391-1253*. Suicide crisis hotline which will give your information (after the phone call) about resources in your local area 24 hours a day.

♦ *CHILDHELP USA National Child Abuse Hotline (800) 4-A-CHILD*. 24 hours a day, toll-free, anonymous phone line providing crisis help for children who are victims of physical, emotional, or sexual abuse. Will tell you about agencies and resources in your community.

Books

♦ *It's Not the End of the World* by Judy Blume, 1972, Dell. A story about a twelve-year-old girl whose parents are getting a divorce.

♦ *How It Feels When Parents Divorce* by Jill Krementz, 1984, Knopf. Real-life stories by young people ages 7-16 about what the divorce experience was like for them.

♦ *The Kids' Book of Divorce: By, For and About Kids* Eric Rofes, editor, 1982, Vintage Books. Written entirely by kids ages 11-14, who tell it like it is—how it feels and how to cope with divorce.

♦ *Divorce Is Not the End of the World* by Zoe, Evan, and Ellen Stern, 1997, Tricycle Press. Zoe (age 15), Evan (age 13), and their mom have a round-table discussion and answer kids' letters about divorce and how to handle all the feelings and changes.

♦ *The Top-Secret Journal of Fiona Claire Jardin* by Robin Cruise, 1998, Harcourt Brace. The funny, honest story of a girl struggling to cope with her parents' divorce, particularly shuttling back and forth between two houses, keeping track of the rules, and all her possessions.

♦ *Coping in a Blended Family* by Jane Hurwitz, 1997, Rosen Publishing Group. This book describes different paths to becoming a blended family, the adjustment to stepparents, step and half siblings, and tips for helping everyone live together.

♦ *"Family Voices," The Other Side of the Closet,* by Amity Pierce Buxton, Ph.D., 1991, John Wiley and Sons. An adult book about marriages in which the husband or wife comes "out of the closet" and reveals that he or she is gay or lesbian. The chapter "Family Voices" tells the stories of teens who have gone through this experience with their parents and are adjusting to a divorce as well as having a gay or lesbian parent.

◆ *Zack's Story: Growing up with Same-Sex Parents* by Keith Elliot Greenberg, 1996, Lerner Publications. A book about eleven-year-old Zack, who describes his life with his mother and her lesbian partner.

Web Sites

You can browse the web to get information on divorce or to find other kids from divorced families:

◆ *Children's Rights Council: http://www.vix.com/crc* This web site includes a place where teens from divorced families can submit poetry, art work, stories, and home pages to share with other teens. It also provides info about taking action or staying informed about social issues of interest to teens.

◆ *StepFamily Foundation - http://www.stepfamily.org*

◆ *StepFamily Association of America http://www.stefam.org*

◆ *Divorce Help - Directory of self-help services http://www.divorcehelp.com*

◆ *COLAGE (Children of Lesbians and Gays Everywhere) www.colage.org*

More Resources

Stepfamilies

For help with a stepfamily, you can contact these national organizations:

♦ *StepFamily Association of America (800) 735-0329 or (402) 477-STEP 650 J Street, Suite 205, Lincoln, NE 68508.* Support group referral, books and tapes on step families. Publishes a book called *Stepfamilies Stepping Ahead.*

♦ *StepFamily Foundation, 333 West End Ave., New York, NY 10023. (800) SKY-STEP or (212) 877-3244.* Also offers short-term phone counseling for a fee, which helps families build communication.

Parents with Problems

If you need help with a parent who has an alcohol, drug, or emotional problem, try:

♦ *National Alcohol and Drug Abuse Hotline (800) 252-6465.* Will refer you to in-patient (live-in) drug and alcohol treatment centers.

♦ *DrugHelp (800) 378-4435.* Provides information and referral to all kinds of substance abuse treatment, including self-help groups, family support, detox, in-patient and out-patient (in the community) counseling.

♦ *Alateen* has support groups for teens with an alcoholic parent. Look up Alateen in your local telephone directory. You can join even if your parent is NOT in Alcoholics Anonymous.

♦ *The National Alliance for the Mentally Ill* (800) 950-

NAMI. Provides information about mental illness, medication, and referral to support groups.

♦ *Connexions (888) 222-1213.* Will provide educational materials and referrals to support groups in your area if someone in your family is depressed.

Kids' Rights

To learn more about your rights, call:

♦ *Children's Rights Council (800) 787-KIDS or (202) 547-6227.* This organization works to guarantee that kids stay in contact with both parents and the extended family when parents divorce. Through state chapters, it helps children by parent education, pamphlets, and legislative action.

ABOUT DIVORCE LAW

Although the legal part of the divorce is your parents' business, all too often you get drawn into the web. The legal words, arguments, and procedures become part of your life. This can make you more worried and confused about what's going to happen. The more you understand about the legal process, the more comfortable you're likely to feel. Here are some questions that teenagers often ask about the legal aspects of divorce.

Q: How long does it take to get a divorce?

A: This can vary from state to state, and from family to family. If your parents are basically in agreement, it may not take too long. But, if your parents are unable to agree on a lot of the divorce arrangements and keep needing to return to court for a judge to make decisions, it could take years for everything to be worked out and for the divorce to be final.

Q: Who makes the decisions about my life, like where I will go to school and who I'm going to live with?

A: One of the things that has to get decided in a divorce is how parents will divide the care, responsibilities, and time spent with their children. This is called *custody* and *visitation*. Usually parents work out these arrangements themselves, but if they can't agree, then the judge will do it.

Whoever has legal custody has the power to decide where you will live, what school you'll go to, and anything else that has to do with your welfare. Often parents will agree to share legal custody so they both can have input into the important decisions regarding their children.

Once custody has been determined, a schedule is made of the time that the kids will spend with each of their parents. This is the *visitation* or *parenting* plan. Because you are a teenager, your parents will probably consult with you about school preferences, activities, and the time you'll spend with each of them. If the arrangements are being made by a judge, he or she would also be concerned with your wishes.

Divorce Dictionary

Sole Custody:
Decision-making power regarding the children goes to either the mom or the dad. Usually, the children live primarily with that parent, and visit the other during specified times.

Joint Custody:
Decision-making power regarding the children is shared by the mother and the father, requiring them both to agree on important child-related decisions such as living arrangements, education, medical procedures, etc. Usually, the children spend more or less equal time with each parent.

Q: How is the money divided? Will there be enough for the things I need?

A: The law requires parents to provide for their children as their first priority. *Child support* is the money paid by one parent to the other each month to cover your basic living expenses. Most parents also work out a payment plan between them for special expenses such as private school, summer camp, or braces. If a parent fails to pay the child support that the court has ordered, the other parent can return to court to require that the payments be made. The amount owed can even be taken out of a parents' salary each month to guarantee that it is paid.

In addition to child support, one of your parents may receive *alimony* (also known as *spousal support or maintenance*) from the other. This money is designed to help both parents keep up a decent standard of living. It provides basic income to a parent who had not been working before the divorce, or who earns a lot less than the other parent. The house and possessions will usually be divided more or less equally between your parents. Sometimes that means the house must be sold so that the money received can be shared.

Q: How are divorce arrangements worked out?

A: Although it may take a while and there can be a lot of arguing along the way, most parents (with the help of their lawyers) are able to work out the details of the divorce without having to go into court. Sometimes the couple uses a mediator to help them work out the arrangements. A mediator is a neutral person (someone who doesn't take sides) who meets with both parents together and helps them to sort out their differences. Once a couple reaches an agreement the arrangements are set forth in a contract known as a *Separation Agreement* or *Settlement Agreement*. If the parties are unable to agree, they will have to go to court where the judge will make decisions for them.

Q: Do I have to go to court or speak to a judge?

A: If your parents are fighting over custody or visitation, the judge will probably want to know how you feel about the situation, how you get along with each parent, and what concerns you may have, but you probably won't have to talk in open court. Either the judge will talk with you privately in a separate room or a *custody evaluation* will be ordered and an evaluator will meet with you privately and make a recommendation to the judge. The thought of meeting with the judge might make you nervous, but most judges will be sensitive to what you are going through. Part of the judge's job is to look out for your welfare.

It is very unusual for any child to be put on the witness stand and asked to provide testimony for or against one parent.

Divorce Dictionary

Separation Agreement

A contract signed by a married couple setting forth the details of their divorce. It deals with issues such as alimony, child support, the division of property, custody, visitation, and any other matters the couple thinks are important. After the Separation Agreement is signed, it is given to the court to be incorporated in the final divorce papers.

Custody Evaluation

When parents cannot agree on custody or one parent feels that the other parent is such a bad influence that it may be dangerous or unhealthy for you to live with that parent, the court will order a custody evaluation. This is a special report that is prepared by the judge or an evaluator appointed by the judge after a number of meetings with each of your parents, with you, and any brothers or sisters, and perhaps with your teachers. After listening to each point of view, the evaluator will make a recommendation to the judge about where the children should live and how much time they should spend with each parent.

Q: Do I need my own lawyer?

A: In most divorces, kids don't go to court or need their own lawyer. Occasionally in a custody or visitation dispute, the judge may feel that neither of your parents is able to focus adequately on the needs of the children. In this circumstance, you may be appointed a lawyer to speak for you in court and to protect your rights and interests.

Q: Do I have to see a parent I don't want to see?

A: It depends. The court usually tries to keep a relationship going between a parent and his or her children, and so almost always orders some kind of visitation. But if the parent has been abusive or emotionally unstable and has put you at serious risk, contact would not be allowed without some kind of protection built in. Sometimes a judge will order *monitored* or *supervised visitation*, in which that parent can visit with you only in the presence of another adult, such as a counselor, a social worker, or even another family member.

If you don't want to see one of your parents, you should definitely tell the judge why. Teenagers have sometimes convinced judges not to insist on visitation.

If you are not in danger, but you feel emotionally upset or turned off around one of your parents, counseling could be helpful. Something may have happened that has caused you to feel alienated, and discussing it can help you decide if trust can be rebuilt. Sometimes the reason you don't want to see one parent is that you're expressing the feelings and wishes of your other parent. Counseling can help you separate your own feelings from your parent's.